j
294.536
MITTER

D0100063

Holidays &
Festivals

HINDU FESTIVALS

Swasti Mitter

Rourke Enterprises, Inc.
Vero Beach, Florida 32964

Holidays and Festivals

Buddhist Festivals
Christmas
Easter
Halloween
Hindu Festivals

Jewish Festivals
Muslim Festivals
New Year
Sikh Festivals
Thanksgiving and Harvest

Text © 1989 Rourke Enterprises, Inc.
PO Box 3328, Vero Beach, Florida 32964

Library of Congress Cataloging-in-Publication Data

Mitter, Swasti, 1939-
   Hindu festivals / Swasti Mitter
      p. cm. – (Holidays & festivals)
   Bibliography: p.
   Includes index.
   Summary: Describes the origins and traditions of Hindu festivals and celebrations.
   ISBN 0-86592-986-6
   1. Fasts and feasts–Hinduism–Juvenile literature. 2.Hinduism–Customs and practices–Juvenile literature. [1. Fasts and feasts–Hinduism. 2 Hinduism–Customs and practices.] I. Title. II. Series: Holidays and festivals.
BL1239.72.M58 1989
294.5'36–dc 19   88-15719
                                                                    CIP
                                                                    AC

Printed in Italy by Tipolitografia G. Canale & C. S.p.A. - Turin

Contents

Hinduism

A seventh-century statue of Ganga, *the river goddess.*

The Hindu religion is one of the most ancient religions in the world. Unlike Islam, Christianity or Buddhism, it had no single founder, but developed gradually over thousands of years, incorporating the teachings of many great religious thinkers. Most Hindus live in India.

An image of Durga, *another form of* Devi, *the Mother Goddess.*

The origins of Hinduism can be traced back to the people who lived in the Indus valley over 4,000 years ago. This is the area that now forms Pakistan and northwest India. From the remains of two ancient cities, Harappa and Mahenjo-Daro, scholars discovered that the inhabitants worshiped a mother goddess and honored trees and animals. Even today, *Devi*, the Mother Goddess, is remembered at many of the important Hindu festivals under a variety of names.

Hinduism is possibly the only religion in the world in which God is often portrayed in female form. The Mother Goddess can be loving and caring; she can also be stern, just like our own mothers.

As with many other cultures, religious festivals in Hindu society provide an opportunity for Hindus to offer thanks for the wonderful things God has given them. They also give the people a chance to feel they are part of Hindu society by participating in rituals and festivals that are centuries old.

A festival procession in Rajasthan.

Many Gods and Many Festivals

Hindus believe essentially in one God – the supreme creator of all living beings. Religious practices are mostly very personal. Through prayers and meditations, Hindus try to be close to God. They believe that God is everywhere, including in themselves, and do not feel that they have to go to a temple in order to be religious. But many people find it difficult to pray to a God that has no name or form.

Hindus pause to offer prayers at one of the many roadside shrines scattered throughout the countryside.

Hindus have overcome the need for imagining God as a person by creating gods and goddesses in mythological stories. These tales have been handed down from ancient times. Hundreds of such gods and goddesses represent the various aspects of the world in which we live. The three main gods are *Brahma* the creator, *Vishnu* the

Hindu families have shrines in their homes.

preserver and *Shiva* the destroyer. *Vishnu* has a number of human forms, or incarnations. There is also *Saraswati*, the goddess of knowledge and learning to whom children pray to help them do well at school; *Lakshmi*, the goddess of wealth, a favorite among the traders and businessmen; and many, many more.

A festival in honor of Saraswati, *the goddess of learning.*

Krishna (*an incarnation of* Vishnu) *defeats an evil serpent.*

Most of India's holidays are religious, and for each of the many gods and goddesses in the Hindu religion there is at least one festival.

Many mythological stories and folk tales are based on love, quarrels and reconciliations among the gods. There are also antigods, who represent wickedness and evil. Gods and goddesses always, eventually, defeat the antigods.

The war between the good and evil forms the central theme of the two most famous Indian epic poems: *Ramayana* and *Mahabarata*. In

10

Crowds watch as performers act out a scene from the epic poem, Ramayana.

Hindu society, these tales bring the assurance of survival and continuity and show that goodness is more powerful than evil. Although these epics were composed many centuries before the birth of Christ, they are still very popular today. They are retold to children and, as we shall see, scenes from them become the subjects of dances, plays and festivals.

You will find a calendar, showing the Hindu months and seasons, and major Hindu festivals on page 45.

11

Dasera

Dasera and Navaratri are celebrations of the Mother Goddess and the triumph of good over evil. Navaratri means "nine nights," and the festival follows the new moon in the month of Bhadra (September), the middle month of the Hindu calendar year. Dasera literally means "tenth day" and is the final day of festivities. It is one of the best-known festivals and is celebrated by Hindus everywhere.

Dasera *celebrated in Kulu, in the far north of India.*

12

Dasera takes place in early autumn (*Sarada*); the sky is then beautifully clear after the monsoon, and the weather is very pleasant, neither too hot nor too cold.

The season also marks a period of leisure following the strenuous agricultural work of the summer and the rainy season. It is the time when the farming community waits hopefully for a good harvest and everyone feels happy.

In this mood of hope and confidence, people try to forget personal disagreements. There is an atmosphere of peace and friendship. The congregational prayers include the expression, *Sarve Jana Sukhino Bhabautu,* which means "Let there be happiness to all living beings."

Many of India's festivals are related to the two harvest seasons of spring and autumn. This is not surprising since the people believe that fertility is a gift from the gods.

At festival time, Hindus decorate their homes and shrines with garlands of flowers.

Forms of Celebrations

Actual celebrations take different forms in different parts of India, but in most places, *Dasera* is the occasion for Hindus to exchange presents and messages of goodwill. Apart from the priestly rituals and religious prayers, it is a season full of communal festivities.

In Gujerat, women dance the famous *Garba* dance to the accompaniment of music. In their colorful clothes, the women look stunningly beautiful.

This water carrier sells holy water from the Ganges River to worshipers.

Dasera is a time for prayer as well as celebration.

In some parts of India, on the ninth day of *Navaratri*, Hindus offer prayers to the tools of their trade – students to their books, craftsmen and workmen to their implements and machines. This occasion is called *Ayudh Puja*, which means "weapon worship."

Hindus seem to feel that the tenth day, *Dasera*, holds a special magical quality. Often on this day young children are ceremonially taught the alphabet. It is also regarded as a lucky day for starting new businesses, or even for buying a new house.

Ramayana

In some parts of north India, the emphasis of the celebration has shifted from the Mother Goddess to *Rama,* an incarnation of *Vishnu.* *Rama* is the hero of the epic story, *Ramayana.* According to this, *Rama's* wife, *Sita,* was kidnapped by a demon and taken to Sri Lanka, the island to the south of India. However, friendly monkeys grasped each other's tails and formed a bridge from the mainland to the island. *Rama,* after praying to *Durga* (*Devi*) for help, crossed the bridge, killed the demon, *Ravana,* and rescued *Sita.* *Rama* is believed to have defeated *Ravana* on this particular day of *Dasera,*

This procession is part of the Ramlila *festivities.*

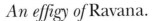

An effigy of Ravana.

and celebrations take place in commemoration of the event. The story is familiar to everyone in India and it is usually dramatized in villages in the form of a pantomime called *Ramlila.* Huge effigies of *Ravana* are made from lattice work covered with paper. At the end of the performance the effigies are burned and blown up with fireworks in the midst of cheering and rejoicing.

Durga Puja

In the eastern part of India, especially in Calcutta, West Bengal and Orissa, Hindus celebrate the victory of the Mother Goddess, *Durga*, over *Mahishasura*, a demon in the shape of a buffalo who wanted to destroy the world.

Sculptors spend months designing and making a clay image of *Durga* in time for the beginning of *Navaratri*. The traditional image shows *Durga* riding a lion. It takes years to train to be a sculptor of these striking clay statues. Some of the artistic skills are handed down from one generation to another and are guarded as a family secret. In orthodox families, *Durga* is sculpted strictly according to the scriptures, but

An image of Durga, *made especially for the* Durga Puja *celebrations.*

in public places, where various youth clubs organize the celebrations, sculptors are allowed to experiment with design and materials.

The last five days of *Navaratri* are the important days for *Durga Puja*. The big cities and towns seem to have a special festive air. The excitement of young boys and girls makes the occasion more of a carnival than a solemn religious affair. The loud music and colorful crowds often meet with the disapproval of the older generation; but for young people, it is seen as a wonderful opportunity to release their energy and high spirits.

Loud music adds to the festive atmosphere in large towns and cities.

The Goddess *Durga* as a Mother and a Daughter

According to the *Puranas*, which belong to the Hindu scriptures, *Durga* is the daughter of the mountain, *Himalaya*, and is married to *Shiva*, one of the three major Hindu gods. In popular tradition, *Durga* comes back to earth for ten days to visit her father's people with four of her children – *Lakshmi*, the goddess of wealth; *Saraswati*, the goddess of learning; *Ganesha*, the elephant-headed god of success; and *Kartikeya*, the god of war. So the demon-slaying, all-powerful Mother Goddess is seen also as a dear daughter of this earth. Indeed, the tenth day of festivities, when the clay image is finally plunged into the Ganges River, is an emotional time for the whole community.

The ceremony surrounding the immersion is very moving because it reminds parents of the temporary visits made by their married daughters, which usually happen only once a year, often at this time. When the daughter returns to her husband's home there is another year's separation before the family is reunited. Before the image of *Durga* is immersed in the Ganges River, the women of each house kiss her goodbye, as if she were their daughter, and ask her to come back again. This is an example of the strong personal bond between a deity and her followers – the joy of meeting and the pain of separation are just as essential a part of the festival as the rituals performed by the priest.

A Hindu woman carries her personal Durga *shrine.*

20

Vijaya Dasami

In western India, the tenth day is called *Vijaya Dasami* (the victorious tenth) rather than *Dasera*. Relatives and friends visit each other and exchange greetings and sweets. If friends and relatives are too far away, Hindus write letters of greeting to them instead.

This is a great day for children, too. They are not scolded or smacked by their parents, even if they are very, very naughty.

Diwali

Diwali is another spectacular religious festival. It is held in late autumn, and on the evening of this particular day, the windows of houses are illuminated by lamps and candles. From a distance and in the darkness, these hundreds of glowing lights are a wonderful sight.

The word *Diwali* is a shortened version of *Dipavali*, which literally means "cluster of lights." Significantly, the celebration takes place on the darkest night of late autumn, usually eighteen days after the celebration of *Dasera*.

The festival of lights is a universal Hindu festival and one of the oldest. However, the mythological theme of the festival, like that of *Dasera*, varies in different areas.

In some parts of Hindu India, *Diwali* is seen as a renewal of life. On this day, old lamps are thrown out and a new lamp fresh from the family potter is put on the manure pile. Besides the fresh start that the ceremony signifies, the new lamps are thought to help the souls of the dead find their way to heaven.

A potter makes new lamps for Diwali.

West Bengal

In West Bengal, the new moon day is dedicated to the worship of *Kali*, the terrifying goddess who destroys all the evils on the earth. She rules over death, and her followers are skeletons and ghosts. Lamps are lit in her honor; in return she promises the renewal of life and justice on earth.

Indeed, the celebration of *Diwali* has an element of magic in it. It is believed that lighting new lamps will drive evil and poverty from the world and welcome better times.

This painting shows the ugly and frightening goddess Kali (Devi *in another form*) *on a battlefield.*

A Raja in his court celebrating Diwali.

Maharashtra

In Maharashtra, *Diwali* is seen as a festival for warding off *King Bali*, the ruler of the underworld. In Hindu mythology, *King Bali* was granted the favor of being the ruler of the earth for one day a year by *Vishnu*, the god who created the world. But it was a conditional favor: *King Bali* could rule only those quarters where no lamp had been lit. Naturally, therefore, people make sure they light lamps everywhere.

Punjab

For Hindus in the Punjab, the festival commemorates the coronation of *Prince Rama*. They also believe that the souls of ancestors come to visit their homes on the new moon day of *Diwali*. Lamps are lit to guide the departed souls on their way. Similar beliefs exist elsewhere in the world – in Japan, the souls of the departed are believed to return to their old homes once a year, and there is a festival, called the feast of the lanterns, to welcome them.

It is interesting to note that the *Diwali* ceremony almost coincides with Halloween, which takes place on October 31, and that Halloween in Europe is also traditionally associated with spirits and the dead.

Diwali – *the festival of lights.*

Gujerat

It is not surprising that *Diwali* is such an important festival in Gujerat, the home of traders who have been successful worldwide. Here, the celebration is associated mostly with *Lakshmi*, the goddess of wealth. This is the day when *Lakshmi* is supposed to have emerged from the milky ocean to bring prosperity to the world. Another version of the story traces the origin to *Vishnu*'s rescue of *Lakshmi* from the evil *King Bali*.

Shopkeepers in Gujerat usually close their accounts at this time. They place their ledgers in front of a picture of *Lakshmi* and pray for better profits in the coming year.

Lakshmi is believed to visit homes that are well lit, so families decorate their homes with flowers and paper chains.

Many people in Gujerat believe the events in the Hindu epic *Ramayana* first inspired this festival. The story goes that *Rama* returned to his kingdom on a *Diwali* day after vanquishing the demon, *Ravana*. *Rama* had been in exile for fourteen years and his followers were so pleased

The blessing of account books at Diwali.

A temple shrine showing Rama *confronting the demoness,* Surpanakha, Ravana'*s sister.*

at the prospect of his return that they lit lamps everywhere to welcome him home.

Diwali is the focal point of a series of religious festivals in Gujerat, lasting for five days. It starts with *Dhan Terash,* the worshiping of wealth by the merchants. Then, for two days, comes the festival of lights. The fourth day, which is that of the new moon, is observed as New Year's day. The day after is a special day on which sisters celebrate the future prosperity and long life of their brothers.

Bhratri Dwitiya

Bhratri Dwitiya is "Brothers' Day" and takes place after the new moon of *Diwali*. It is an important festival both in Gujerat and in eastern India. Girls perform rituals to ward off the power of *Yama,* the god of death, from the lives of their brothers. Brothers accept the gifts showered on them by their loving sisters and offer them presents in return. Sisters rub the foreheads of their brothers with sandalwood powder and chant good wishes:

> With this, I forestall the entry of *Yama,* the god of death, into your life. May your life be full of golden future.

The occasion brings brothers and sisters closer together. It also provides a good opportunity to plan a big family banquet.

A sister wishes her brother good luck on Brothers' Day.

Raksha Bandhan

There is another day in the year that is as much a sister's day as a brother's. It takes place on a full moon day in the month of *Sravana*, which is August in our calendar. Girls tie a *rakhi*, or amulet, made of silk thread around their brothers' wrists. It is believed to act as a charm, to protect them from evil during the coming year. The gift of the *rakhi* also involves a claim by the girl that the brother act as her protector. He gives her a present in return, and the more generous he is on this day, the greater the feast she will prepare for him on *Bhratri Dwitiya*.

As a special favor, a man can receive a *rakhi* from a women even if he is not her brother, but only if he vows to love her like a sister. In this way, exchanging *rakhis* becomes the center of communal festivity as well as of sibling love.

A family banquet. Here, the food is served on banana leaves.

Holi

Holi is a famous and very popular spring festival in northern India. It is celebrated for five days and provides an excuse for everyone to have great fun. Although the festival is meant to be in honor of the minor goddess, *Holika,* it is more a celebration of the spring wheat harvest. Bonfires are built, people play outdoor games and everybody is encouraged to be boisterous. They throw red powders and colored water at each other, not just over their friends but over strangers too, so it's wise to wear old clothes!

These Hindus have been throwing colored powders and water over each other to celebrate Holi.

A Maharajah playing Holi *with the ladies of his court.*

The *Holi* bonfire is considered sacred. When it is being built, all the families in the neighborhood contribute fuel for it. The ashes of the fire are streaked on the forehead to bring good luck in the year ahead.

This Hindu spring festival can be compared with the harvest festivals of ancient Europe, and even more with the riotous Roman festival of *Saturnalia.* This took place in December, and everyone was allowed to make fun of many things normally respected and held sacred throughout the rest of the year.

Holi is celebrated in a different way in the rice-growing area of eastern India. There, on the day of the full moon, the legendary love of

Radha *and* Krishna.

the god *Krishna* (another incarnation of *Vishnu*) and his beloved *Radha* is re-enacted, to the accompaniment of traditional songs. Swings are made of flowers, as *Radha* and *Krishna* were supposed to have played together on a swing on that day.

Throwing colored powders at each other is also seen as a remembrance of the playful frolics of *Radha* and *Krishna*. In some parts of India, in fact, the festival is first and foremost a celebration of their love.

32

Ratha Jatra

In eastern parts of India, the chariot festival is the focal point of the annual cycle of religious festivals. The celebration takes place primarily in Puri, Orissa, where there is a big and beautiful temple to *Jagannath* (a form of Krishna). The name *Jagannath* literally means the God or the lord of the universe. Hindus make a pilgrimage to the temple whenever they get a chance, but it

A Hindu family on a pilgrimage.

A chariot festival in southern India.

Statues of Jagannath *(right),*
his sister Subhadra *(middle)*
and brother Balaram *(left).*

is considered very special if the pilgrim can be there at *Ratha Jatra*.

Every year, on a specific day of the rainy season (June–July), the image of *Jagannath* is carried out of the temple in a huge wooden chariot. The image is bedecked with flowers and jewels and looks most impressive. The chariot is nearly 45 feet (14 meters) high and has sixteen wheels that are 7 feet (2 meters) across. Thousands of people pull the chariot along by ropes, and they believe that God will reward them for their help. At one time some pilgrims used to throw themselves under the wheels of the chariot in the belief that they would go straight to paradise. From the Indian name for this chariot, the word *juggernaut* has come into the English language to describe a huge truck or other object that will crush anything in its path.

Alongside *Jagannath* sit his brother, *Balaram*, and his sister, *Subhadra*. Hindu gods are believed to be very fond of their family, just as Hindus are. Brothers and sisters play very important roles in a Hindu family, and images of gods and goddesses often reflect this feeling of love.

Folk Festivals

Most religious festivals take place according to the strict instructions of religious scriptures. The priests are almost always of Brahmin caste – the highest caste in Hindu society.

But there are many other festivals that belong to particular villages and localities. They are folk

At festival time, villagers dress in colorful clothes, play music and dance.

festivals and are different in nature from the major religious festivals and vary from region to region.

Folk festivals are only partly religious in character. Although there are priests, they are not necessarily Brahmins. The rituals often have an element of magic – some rituals are meant to ward off the evil eye, for example. Epidemics, such as cholera, often play havoc in village communities where medical supplies are scarce. In desperation, villagers try to please the Mother

Sometimes temple images, like this statue of Hanuman *the monkey god, are taken around the village streets in a cart.*

Goddess, whose fury, they believe, is the cause of such a disease. In southern India she is called *Mariamma*, but village people call her by different names in different parts of India.

Joyous folk festivals often celebrate the agricultural year. In the month of *Agrahayana* (November–December) thanksgiving celebrations take place. In the rice-growing regions of northern India, offerings of newly cooked rice are made to village gods. The celebration is called *Navanna* (new rice). In the south there is a similar festival, with the boiling of new rice, which takes place in January. It is called *Pongal* (boiled new rice) and lasts for three days.

Pongal *rice is offered to the gods.*

Family Festivals

Praying for the well-being of the family is often a festive occasion. No priest is called in to perform the ceremonies – festivals are performed entirely by women, who pray for the long life and happiness of their husbands and children.

One of the best known of such festivals is called *Sasthi Puja* and involves prayers to the goddess of fertility. Women worship the banyan tree. As the tree has many roots, so the women hope to have many children.

These Hindu women have gathered together to pray for their families.

Hindu Festivals outside India

Over the centuries, Hinduism spread eastward from India. Some countries adopted Buddhism or Islam, but Hindu influences still remain in Nepal, Thailand, Malaysia and the island of Bali in Indonesia.

A huge chariot at a Nepalese festival.

In Bali, the mountains are believed to be the dwelling places of the gods, while the sea is the home of the antigods. For this reason the sea is feared by the Balinese, who rarely venture far from the shore. Long processions, bearing offerings to the antigods, are a common sight on the south coast of the island.

In the last hundred years, many Indians have emigrated. As a result, the West Indies, Trinidad and Tobago, Mauritius, Kenya, Uganda and South Africa all have sizable Indian populations. Wherever Indians went, they took with them their rich and colorful religious and cultural traditions.

A long procession, bearing offerings, on the coast of Bali.

Celebrations of Hindu festivals in countries like the United States and Britain are relatively recent, since Indians only began to settle in these countries in the mid-1950s. There was a shortage of skilled and unskilled workers at that time, and many people from India were attracted by the higher standards of living in the West.

About three-quarters of a million Hindus now live in North America, and over half a million live in Europe. Many of the nearly 300,000 Hindus living in Great Britain came from East Africa. Although many of the Hindus living in the West have never been to India, Hindu

English schoolgirls get ready to perform the Garba *dance. It is usually performed in Gujerat at* Dasera.

tradition is still very important to them. It is not surprising, then, that some of the festivals are celebrated in America and in Europe with as much grandeur as they are in India.

In many ways, these celebrations abroad give children of Hindu origin a sense of identity in a Christian world; while for American and European children, they provide an opportunity to glimpse an old, rich, yet non-Christian culture.

We are fortunate to live in a society where so many different cultures and religions exist together. It enriches experience for all of us.

Diwali *celebrated in a Hindu home in Britain.*

The Hindu Calendar

In India, events such as Republic Day are reckoned by the same calendar as in the West, but for religious festivals, dates are determined according to the Hindu calendar. In this system, a year is divided into twelve months according to the movements of the moon, and each month is

Whatever the time of year, Hindu festivals always attract colorful crowds.

Seasons	Calendar Months	Hindu Festivals		
Summer (*Grishma*)	**Vaishakha** (*Apr–May*)	New Year (in most of India)		
	Jaistha (*May–June*)			
Rainy (*Varsha*)	**Asadha** (*June–July*)	*Ratha Jatra* (Chariot Festival)		
	Sravana (*July–Aug*)	*Raksha Bandhan*		
Early autumn (*Sarada*)	**Bhadra** (*Aug–Sept*)			
	Aswin (*Sept–Oct*)	*Navaratri* and *Dasera* *10 days*	*Durga Puja*	
Late autumn (*Hemanta*)	**Kartik** (*Oct–Nov*)	*Diwali* (Festival of Lights) *5 days*	*Bhratri Dwitiya* (Brothers' Day)	
	Agrahayana (*Nov–Dec*)	*Navanna* (New rice)		
Winter (*Sit*)	**Paus** (*Dec–Jan*)			
	Magh (*Jan–Feb*)	*Pongal*		
Spring (*Vasanta*)	**Phalgun** (*Feb–Mar*)	*Holi* (Festival of Colors)		
	Chaitra (*Mar–Apr*)			

divided into two halves. The first half begins on the day after the new moon and is called "bright half." The second half begins on the day after the full moon and is called "dark half."

Since the calendar in the West is fixed by the movement of the sun, the dates according to the Hindu calendar do not always correspond to those in the Western calendar. Hence you may find the festival of *Dasera* taking place some years at the end of September and in other years at the beginning of October.

Glossary

Amulet A bracelet or a piece of jewelry worn as protection against evil.

Antigod As gods represent the powers of goodness, so antigods represent the powers of evil. In Hindu mythology, antigods are cousins of gods.

Brahmin A member of the highest or priestly caste in the Hindu caste system.

Caste Ancient Hindus believed that Hindu society could be divided into four classes or castes – priests, warriors, traders and peasants – and that a person's position was decided by being born into one of these four groups.

Commemoration A ceremony or service in memory of a person or event.

Consort A partner or companion, especially a husband or wife.

Deity A god or goddess.

Effigy A dummy figure of someone, usually made fun of and sometimes hung up or burned in public.

Emigrate To go from one country or region to settle in another.

Epidemic An outbreak of a disease that spreads to affect very many people.

Evil eye A look or glance, superstitiously thought to have the power of injuring.

Incarnation A god in human form.

Monsoon The rainy season.

Mythology Legends and popular stories handed down from earlier times, usually concerning gods and goddesses.

Orthodox Holding the views and beliefs that are most usually held.

Pilgrimage A journey to a shrine or other sacred place.

Puja The main Hindu form of worship, often involving a ceremony in which flowers and food are placed before a god and prayers said.

Puranas Hindu stories that tell of the birth and deeds of Hindu deities.

Reconciliation To become friendly again after a quarrel.

Ritual A set way of performing a religious service.

Sibling A person's brother of sister.

Further Reading

If you would like to find out more about Hindu festivals and the Hindu religion, look for these books at your library:

I Am a Hindu by Manju Aggarwal (Watts, 1985)

The Hindu World by Patricia Bahree (Silver Burdett, 1982)

Hinduism by V. P. Kavitkar (Watts, 1986)

Cradle Tales of Hinduism (Vendanta Press, 1972)

Way of the Hindu (Dufour)

Index

Acknowledgments

The publisher would like to thank all those who have provided pictures on the following pages: Camerapix Hutchison Library cover, 12, 15, 25, 30, 41, 43; Bruce Coleman Ltd 19, 44 (Charles Henneghien); Jane Edmonds 6; The Evening Argus, Brighton 42; Preben Sejer Kristensen 8; Swasti Mitter 28; Ann and Bury Peerless 4, 5, 7, 9, 10, 11, 13, 14, 16, 17, 18, 20, 21, 22, 24, 26, 27, 29, 31, 32, 33, 34, 35, 38, 43; 23 by courtesy of the Board of Trustees of the Victoria and Albert Museum; Wayland Picture Library 36; ZEFA 37, 39, 40.